Back To Being A Woman.

Also By Katherine A. Rayne

Back To Being A Woman

(Without Changing the Man)

There's a Light at the

End of the Tunnel. *You.*

by Katherine A. Rayne

www.BackToBeingAWoman.com

Published November 2014   Designed by Katherine A. Rayne

Contact Email Address: Katherine@KatherineARayne.com

Manufactured in the United States of America

ISBN #: 978-0-9910552-2-7

Dedicated to

Brandon and Kendra

the shiny lights that live within my heart and

in my life

who have shown me how precious and

miraculous life is.

Introduction

My Bio

Katherine A. Rayne

Birth   Katherine Ann, born the youngest of four daughters in Alberta, Canada
Height   5'2" (almost)
Family   Parents: Alma (housewife) and Glen (conservationist engineer)
Sisters   Donna, Lynn and Karen
Childhood Pets   Pepi (black "regal-acting" poodle), Squeakie (very messy guinea pig). And then there was Bimbo...mutt and most loving, beloved buddy ever. Add in some hermit crabs, a large, muscular stolen rat (ick...not my idea). I think we named him Harold. Plenty of goldfish and guppies destined for the toilet, finches (Beepbeep and Twirpy), some gerbils, very large and wartish toads (I'd play with them as if they were "Ken" with my Barbie dolls since I never had a Ken doll), and the typical frogs, tadpoles and lizards (all experimental, of course) and even some really cute little white mice saved from the pet store food supply. And last but not

least, sea monkeys. (They really did hatch.)

Relocated to Sunny Florida in the 70's after my parents divorced.

Met my future husband (as well as future ex) in late 1987, married in 1991, left banking a few months before my first child, a son, born in 1993. Second child, a daughter, was born in 2003.

Mother and Father, both deceased in 2004. My mother was diagnosed in 2001 with cancer. She was blessed to live another 3 ½ years with family always close by. Her last ten days were spent in the hospital in July of 2004. Received news during that ten days that my father (residing in Canada), was in the hospital after diagnoses and immediate surgery of cancerous brain tumor. (No, I'm not kidding…ridiculous, right?) My mother passed first in July, then my father one month later.

Went on a (emotional) journey soon after.

:)

My Comforts

Chocolate covered cranberries (yuuummmm)

Putting pajamas on after a long day

Reading

Writing

Iced-chai tea lattes (as in: "what do you MEAN you drank the last of it???")

The BEACH

Walking

Even better, walking on the BEACH

Eating outdoors

Movies and popcorn together

Browsing used books in thrift stores

My bed

Music (I would have gladly kissed the feet of the inventor of the iPod)
A REALLY good hamburger (especially if it has pickles)
An even better tasting steak
(which reminds me…red wine)
My kids, my kids, my kids.

My Discomforts
Rollercoasters
Flying
Motorcycling
Cold weather
Seeing grown daughters lunching out with their mothers
Cockroaches (ICK)
Mosquitoes

My Miscellaneous

First job My aunt's t-shirt shop in 8th grade
First kiss 13 (and it was icky)
First love At sweet 16
First car blue firebird (me and the bank)
First home away from home At 17, mom moved me in with my sister while mom dealt with an illness
First home owned At 20 years old, a teeny tiny condo
First pet after moving out on my own Beau; part Chihuahua, part Yorkshire, part human. He died at the ripe old age of 17 a few years back.

First cat I was not a cat person, but didn't know why not after having one. Tiger cat, Snickers (speaking of "regal-acting").

Current pets Muffin, a sweet little Papillion who made me break my promise to myself of swearing I'd never get another dog, and a Beta fish named Petey who lives in a teeny tiny space and gets my pity every time I walk by him. My daughters' hamster, named Henry and a Beta fish named Rockstar that is my classroom pet. He officially belongs to my preschool students but lives with me at home until our Pet Week.

table of contents

one

own your moments

The cracks that happen in our lives only make us brighter. The challenges break us open, and out comes our light. The more cracks, the more light. I don't know about you, but my light is pretty stinkin' shiny. :) I'm aiming high! Embrace your light and shine it onto your days. Make sure that everyone has to wear sunglasses when you walk by!

There are so many tragedies in life and some of us end up owning more than our fair share. To take them on, we first have to own them. Allow them to settle into our lives and into our bones, then deal with them, live through them and find the lesson in them. Tragedies happen to help us uncover our weaknesses and limitations. We are forced to find our interior light which becomes our life compass. We will use

it to shine our way through the dark.

So put on your big-girl-panties, and

your sunglasses, and Shine-Own! You

are the light in your dark!

Making the most of your moments will help make the most out of you. From the day we are born, life is already planning out our highs and lows for us. We hit so many roadblock lows. We don't understand why we keep hitting them, but we are there to shine. We won't feel like it. We will feel like shutting down and closing off the outside world and sitting in the dark. But once we've rinsed our hearts clean with our tears and pushed ourselves up from the depression-inducing sofa, we need to dig for the lesson. There are always lessons, and I don't want you to miss even one. Lessons are what give you your light. The more cracks in your soul, the more light that seeps out. So what are you waiting for? Start bleeding your light. Stop holding it in and suffocating it. Own it and shine it! *Shine-own!* You are enough. Who you are, as you are, you're enough. It's wonderful to have family to support you, and friends to go through the valleys with you. We need to depend on others in order to live a sane life. Having support and love and shoulders to cry on is vital. But even if everyone you depended on left tomorrow, as you are, you are abundant on your own. You have everything you

There's a Light at the End of the Tunnel. You.

need to do what needs to be done and to get through the dark on your

own. This world belongs to you, too. Along your journey, you can

pull ahead through life as far as you want to or you can just lag

behind everyone else and watch them live in the light that we are all

entitled to. So forgive, accept, love, smile, give, live, embrace, own

and shine. You own those traits already. Use them blatantly and with

everyone.

Miss Takes

I was a mistake as an embryo. Not planned for and not wished-upon-a-star for. I was a determined-to-be-born sperm that tail-ended a family of three other daughters, so of course dad wished for a boy. Without anyone wishing for me, as I am, I still made it here. And even though my embryo was a mistake, I am not. The universe and God don't make mistakes. They make life and birth and death and imperfection and perfection and miracles and tragedy and beauty. Even their ugly is beauty. But there are no mistakes. To waste those non "Miss Takes," is such a big mistake. I was put here to make differences. Plurally. And the differences need to linger on after I'm only a light. The fact that I am writing this means that I have fingers and eyesight. We know for sure that I have a brain. Double-Blessing. That's all I need. Now I am capable to make differences. To think, to grow, to learn, to lead, to move forward and to be abundant. To be enough. I am here for me but I am also here for you. I get to aim my Flash (of) Light where ever I want to.

There are times that I feel the emotion that tells me "I'm not enough" creeping in. Even though I absolutely know that I am. But they say we're not supposed to feel those ones. We are "treated" for having sad, depressed, negative thoughts. We are given therapy, medications and we are shamed. Remember, though, that it is just advice from other "Miss Takes" and I've decided that I know myself better than they do. I need those emotions. I've learned to trust them and to own them, whether they are negative or positive. I'm also very stubborn so I won't stop feeling them, anyway. Eventually I shake off my negative ones, but only after I figure out what it is that I'm shaking off. Life is twists and turns and upside downs. Those moments were tailor made for me. They are what help direct me from my point A to point B. So I feel them and own them. And I never dull them or sugarcoat them. An emotional-diet rich in sugar is not healthy. Dulling them dulls my light. Emotions don't scare me because they can't harm me. Even the tough ones. I'm not me without them.

When I was a newly formed little being fresh outside of my mother's womb, others' emotions began to form mine. I felt, saw and heard their reactions to life as it happened, and so my judgments became based on what I learned from them. What I also learned along the way is that some of those emotions belonged to someone else and I didn't have to keep them. I could discard them or keep them. I control me. Miss Takes takes control!

Emotions are strong, but I am stronger. No one misses out on hurting during their lifetime, but the emotions we feel are normal. They happen, and then the cracks open us up and make us stronger and brighter. Sit next to your emotions instead of in them. Have conversations with them as if they are a friend. Tell them what's best for them, and for you. Be understanding but selfish. Give them space and the best advice that you know. Use your intuition. It's there for a reason and it knows what it's talking about. Let it walk you through your moments. Then own them. Take and own what life doesn't want you to Miss out on. Be Miss Takes and all.

I am Miss Takes. Not only in physical form from birth, but I make lots of mistakes. I hate making mistakes and the older I get, the more I make. I go through the dark like everyone else so I keep my Flash Light at my side for when I need it and I use it often.

The weight of your life does not have to influence your path. Your path as of this moment is clear and open to the direction that you want it to take.

When we get thrown into a boat of treacherous waters, life yells at us, "Sink or swim!" Don't forget to yell back, "I'm in a LIFE boat!"

I'm floating!" Float for as long as you need to. Floating is riding with the tide. It's not even as involved as treading. Treading is kicking and paddling. Float and use your Flash Light for as long as you need to. When you're ready to stop floating, start flying!

When I think of the darkness in my life, the worst is my mom's death. My three sisters and I watched her slowly pass away in the hospital over a period of ten days. Thank God for my sisters because my Flash Light ran out of batteries.

My mom stayed strong with cancer for three and a half years but this was it. It was ten days of extreme sadness and wondering how I was going to survive without her. I was also wondering why I wasn't crying 24/7. I had dry spells of disbelief and quiet. One morning I experienced a brief moment of amnesia about the reason we were there while sitting in the hospital cafeteria with my sisters. One of us made a joke and I was surprised to hear myself laugh. Through those ten days, I found myself thinking about death, but the most memorable thoughts are the thankful ones. Sitting next to her bed, staring at her as she slept, I was thankful for each breath she took. I remember being so thankful that I had her for so many years. She had beat cancer twenty years before. Sitting there next to her, I realized that I'd spent every single holiday with her. I found myself somehow counting blessings. But forefront on my mind was *how will I survive without her?* Ten days went by fast with more and more cracks forming.

And then there was the chocolate cake. Nurses would come into my mom's room to check her vitals and care for her while we surrounded her, and you braced yourself to hear the nurse's news about her failing body. When a nurse spoke, I listened closely. All of my senses were attuned to taking in her words, not with hope but with dread. One day we spoke about the food in the cafeteria with a regular nurse and she advised us not to miss out on the delicious chocolate cake. I heeded her words as if it were lifesaving advice.

Chocolate cake is Comfort food with a capital C. From that moment on, I sat with their chocolate cake as if it was a life boat. I had quickly lost weight while my mom was in the hospital, but after she passed away, I replaced her with chocolate cake. So many things in life are fixable. I say that to my preschool students when they are upset about a problem. *"Everything is fixable."* But your mom dying is not fixable. You can't do a thing to fix it or to change it. It was easy to relate my mom to food, because she nurtured me with it for so many years. After she died, I gained the freshman-15-pounds-in-the-school-of-losing-moms. It became my Flash Light. My kids, family, friends and Chocolate Cake got me through. It's important to find pleasure through hard times and chocolate cake was one of mine.

During her funeral, I found myself smiling on occasion. Years before, I had attended a funeral and saw the widow smile on occasion during her husbands' funeral. I couldn't imagine where she had found one. But it happened to me. Whenever I saw close friends or family walk into the room and when the minister and his soothing form arrived, their presence brought out my lost smile.

I also discovered a new me at my mom's funeral. The DVD player malfunctioned near the beginning of the memorial video we put together. A funeral parlor full of people stared at a blank screen for ten minutes before it was working again. Before my mom's death, something like that would have rattled me. It would have worried me and stressed me out. As I sat there for those ten minutes, I realized I wasn't worried. I wasn't bothered. I didn't even care. I had just begun living a life without my mom in it. And that to me was the worst kind of tragedy. And so far I was successful at living through it. If I can live through my mom's death, I can certainly handle an electrical issue. It was such a small matter compared to what I was dealing with in my life; death. That malfunctioning DVD player made me realize that there is so much in the world that we worry about that isn't worth worrying about. I'd always loved the saying, *"if God will bring you to it, he will bring you through it"* and now I was living it. He'd brought me through my mom's death and I was

still standing, smiling on occasion, even laughing and eating

delicious chocolate cake. I still had my Flash Light and it had new

batteries.

I'm intentionally leaving out all of that very awful, gut-wrenching-

losing-your-mother moments. There are so many. Now her

memories make me smile, but it took two years for that to finally

happen. My mom and my pillow will be the only ones that know the

most drastic moments I have experienced since her passing. She's

my Guardian Angel. Ten years later I still miss her terribly, but if

anyone deserves to live in Heaven, it's my mom. That makes living

without her a bit easier.

If we didn't have moments where we were barely hanging on,

scraping bottom and not knowing what direction was up, we

wouldn't be living. Difficulties grow your soul. Own them, because they are now a part of you. Experiencing tragedy creates cracks in us that allow those Flashes (of) Light to shine out. With each difficult experience, the crack grows and allows more light. Each time it opens wider, the light shines brighter until it is no longer a Flash (of) Light but a constant one. Go for broke and let the cracks form!

Hidden in my words and stories within these chapters are moments and incidents from finding and owning my own moments. They are not tragedies but simple moments in life that required a bit of my Flash Light. Use it anywhere and at any time and remember that it's always there. Using it strengthens it. Combine your heart and your light and you will be light-hearted. Don't Miss out on Taking from life the opportunities and possibilities that you are given just by being born. Recognize and own them. Shine-Own!

Love, Miss Takes

two

healthy you

Keeping It "Together"

When summer begins, Orlando comes to mind as one way to celebrate the warm season. The parks there are close enough for a two-day escape without making me delirious with the stress that vacations create. There's no plane ride or an airport involved and I'll be home again before you can count to three (days).

But there is backlash when you mention SeaWorld. So much so that when I think of SeaWorld, I think of the backlash. Many opponents are upset about how they contain their sea animals and the cruelty of it, but I admit it remains one of my favorite parks to take my kids to during the wide-open summers. I have years of breezy strolling-through-the-park memories from our visits.

There are few lines in SeaWorld; just crowds moving across the park together and finding seats together and oo-ing and ahhh-ing together and getting soaked together before herding off towards another show together.

It's never been a place of rushing. The crowd moves in unison in the same direction, simplifying the task of walking alongside strollers and determined two-year-olds wanting to walk outside of their mom's sweaty arms. It makes what could be a long, hot day less rushed and chaotic.

When I am tired from the togetherness and walking, we follow the map to the children's play area. I'm exhausted but my daughter is bubbling with the excess energy she drank in while sitting still during the shows. Our visit last year went the same as it always does; herds, togetherness, feasting, ice-cold watering holes in the summer-heat temperatures, and then the peaceful relaxing playground. But while in my peaceful whatalovelydaythishasbeen haze last year, out of my focus came a woman wearing a SeaWorld shirt screeching at me as she appeared from the shadows of the slides and bridges' darkness. First just a distant sound but as she came closer, I heard her desperation asking me to tell my daughter not to run on the playground. Did I fall asleep into a funky heatstroke induced dream? I listened intently as she explained, with her dust of distress coming off of her in sprays, why she didn't want my daughter running. There were young ones on the playground that she was worried about and was asking the bigger children not to run.

I wasn't sure how to answer her so instead I watched the angst of her past few days (or years?) come out of her orifices. Puffs of her dust kept coming from her clothes and pores and out of her ears and I watched it settle around her, never touching my sweaty skin.

My daughter now next to me, taking this image in with me, two

against one. We were both quiet and intact while Mrs. SeaWorld

opened her vents and spewed on us. I let her. I saw it in her eyes and

in her hands and her shoulders and in her dust trail. She was spent.

How many hours had she been out in the hot sun with 1.2 million

children, and for how many days? Also there beside her, still and

invisible, were whatever problems she had going on at home. I

waited for the frustration and the anger and the nerves and the worry

to settle at her feet in front of me.

Quiet, her sad eyes now looked to me for a response, as did my

daughters'. My daughter now thinking she was in quantum trouble

because she had caused the playground lady to lose herself.

I simply said, "okay." Mrs. SeaWorld was expecting my sympathy

and rebuttal but I was still in my peaceful slumber looking through

her cloud of spent dust and wanting her to feel better. She blinked the fog from her eyes and found herself standing alone in her gloom. She squirmed her explanation of concern for the little ones once more before lunging off to monitor a playground full of children at full throttle.

I looked to my confused daughter, who was open-mouthed curious of the next words out of my mouth. *"You're fine, hon. Don't let her ruin your fun."*

She decompressed after I spoke, then felt safe to judge and convict the playground woman and her silly request. I realized that she didn't see the same woman as I had so I explained that she was probably ready for a break (or a vacation) and that staying on the other end of the playground was a good idea. Its vastness would make that easy and would allow me to go back to my peaceful state.

Mrs. SeaWorld has never left my thoughts completely. She always revisits when thoughts of Sea World and backlash do. Maybe I could have said something to comfort her. I could have asked her to sit down and talk, or offered to get her some water, but I think she got what she needed; an "okay."

As she walked away with her own thoughts and feelings about what had happened, she has probably never forgotten that day either. I hope that it's a moment in time that she can forgive herself of. Life can trip us up sometimes, but if we wait for the dust to settle, we'll see clearly again.

What Stop Sign?

There are so many things in life that "stop us" from moving forward. Insecurity. Judgment. Being afraid. Exhaustion. Worry.

We can see them coming from a mile away, but each and every time we stop cautiously, sheepishly and diligently, always politely allowing the worry to go on ahead in front of us. We don't know yet what's on the other side, but we're afraid of it already. *Oh dear. Here comes one of those moments. I think I'll stop here and take a break while I ponder all of the things that could go wrong.*

I had a great aunt who had a brain tumor removed many years ago. Along with the tumor, the doctors removed her worry. Literally. I don't know about you, but don't great aunts *already* say the darndest things?! You can imagine what thoughts came out of her mouth. No care, no worry, always with a teasing grin. Almost always turning my six-year old mouth into an OVAL. But along with the silence in the room that often followed her comments, my guess is that many of the adults around her were wishing that they didn't have worry holding them back, either.

What if our minds didn't use worry? And didn't know worry. Would our instincts kick in hard and drive us to where we are supposed to be *sooner* and with less of the gray hairs?

My daughter has the worry wart. Its hidden most of the time but it comes out when she's home and feels safe. To make her feel better, I try to make her think of the worst thing that could happen and how we could handle it if it actually happened. Every time I remember to use this tactic, it puts her sweet mind at ease.

Many times the worst is not awful. It is livable. It is workable. It's get-around-able. So instead of going around it or letting it go ahead of us, we need to just plow through it.

Be *curious* about what's on the other side of it. And eager. And forget the worry wart that grows in between your intelligence and sense of humor. Disengage it. Go through this world by barging through your octagon signs leaving oval signs in your path!

A definition of worry: verb 1. to torment oneself with, or to make oneself suffer from disturbing thoughts; fret.

Please note *"torment oneself."* It means that we do it to ourselves! We create worries with our imagination. Use your imagination to conjure up positive occurrences instead! Why think about all the *bad* things that can happen when you could be thinking about all of the good things that can happen? Break the habit of thinking about the problems that might arise and create a new habit of imagining all of the good things that are possible. Plunge through your stop signs when they start popping up. You'll go further.

Worrying is Stupid…

Worrying is Stupid. It's like walking around with an umbrella waiting for it to rain. -Wiz Khalifa

I came across this quote today and decided I must share it. I want to relieve women of worry it seems, so this comparison of worry to an unnecessary umbrella is inspiration for me (and my worries). I have never heard of Mr. Wiz Khalifa until today, but after dutifully Googling him, I found that "Wiz" is his nickname because of his wisdom, and that he likes cannabis. I find his words inspiring enough to quote, regardless of his habits. Because it is truthful. I know this because of my habits. A worrier.

I want our inner light to calm and suffocate our worries because it really is wasteful. Our energies can be better utilized if we think, breathe and focus on something better. Something more useful.

In my book, Back To Being A Woman (Without Changing the Man), one of my chapters discuss confidence within ourselves in all areas, including with our physical traits. We each know what we dislike about our body. Big nose, small breasts, thick thighs, surgical scars. I compare worry to the negative focus we put on our physical traits that we aren't happy with. Stop focusing on those traits of yourself that you don't like. Don't let them overshadow all of your best features. Let your good traits stand up and shine. And the same with how we worry. It does not have to be a part of your day. You can shove it off to the side so that your intelligence and common sense can come through and ideas of what your day will entail can push forward in its place. Why worry about that meeting? Why worry about what's for dinner? Why worry that you didn't get to the gym once again? Why worry that you are running late in traffic? That ten minutes of worry won't fix it for you or improve upon it. You will still be in the same dilemma as before you began to worry. What if you focus on how you are going to limit that situation in the future? Set a plan. Or just let them go. The moments will pass. Think about better things. Acknowledge that dinner will still taste good, no matter what you decide to have. Remember that the meeting will happen, ready or not. Take it in stride.

Our days will always have challenges. Accept the challenges, including the unplanned ones. Have the confidence that you will make it through, just as you have every other day of your life.

They are such small matters in the context of life. Life is so much bigger than the worry we create for ourselves. Soooo much bigger. Create a habit of positives. Look for the good, even in the bad. Ask yourself what is the silver lining and reflect it onto your day.

Being Fit Begins You

I dread vacations. I always enjoy them once I'm there, but it's the preparations that deter me from smiling for the days leading up to them. The planning stages. Don't forget to put the mail on hold. Call the vet to schedule the boarding of Fluffy (that really IS his name but not what we call him). Stop the newspaper delivery. All laundry must first be done before packing begins. Dreadful.

Then, I have to fly. In the SKY. Ugh.

The path to being healthier feels the same way. Meal planning, grocery list, grocery shopping. Join (and pay for) the gym or start the planning of workouts. I don't know what half of those exercises are that I find on lists of suggestions. Even the diagrams are confusing to me. Does my knee go forward or stay under my shoulder? How far down should I crouch? *Where* does my arm go? So let's not bother with the latest diet trend or exercise machine. Let's use our heads. Make a list of your favorite foods including fruits and vegetables. A long list. Now cross off anything that won't make you healthier than what you are right now. By now, there are a few million of us that know what's healthy for our bodies and what's not, without the help of a magazine article.

Then serve your vegetable portions larger and the other items (proteins and carb items) as smaller portions. Another way? Keep eating what you already eat, but put half of what you would normally eat onto your plate. And eat no later than 7:00 p.m. That's a hard one for me, too.

Make sure that you have something in the kitchen to reach for

instead of food after 7:00 p.m. A deck of cards, a journal, the needle

and thread for those five shirts sitting in the laundry room, nail

polish remover and polish, a sketching pad and pencils. Even that

smartphone or iPad. Potato chips would leave grease on your device,

after all.

Exercise. Ick. Unless you are in the habit of it. If you are in the habit

of it, it's no longer ick. I'm not very good at working out at home.

The laundry is always calling out my name or the thirty other odd

jobs awaiting my attention, so I'm very easily distracted. But how

much time do we spend in front of the TV? Especially at night.

Pajamas on? Perfect. When the commercials come on, pick an

exercise. Any exercise. Your choice…the first thing that comes to

mind. And do it until the commercial ends. If you feel embarrassed

doing it in front of family, make them do it with you. Take turns

picking out the exercise for each commercial. Going for broke? Do

the exercises during the SHOW instead of the commercials. Either way, make sure you're going to be sore within the next 48 hours.

Then you will know it's worth it. You can make those things in the

mirror that you don't like disappear. Make this a continued pattern.

Not a chore for a week or two. You might even surprise yourself and

turn off the TV some nights and get your music going. Don't worry

about how many repetitions for each exercise. Repeat the exercise

until the commercial (or song) ends.

I'm not worried about how much you weigh. It's about feeling

better. Feeling better physically. Feeling better about daily choices.

Feeling better about what you had for dinner. Feeling better about

walking away from the bakery in the grocery store. Doing those little

things that give you an emotional moment that says, *how proud am*

I?! Over and over again.

Begin You. Because if you're too busy thinking about those things

that you see in the mirror that you don't like, you're taking away from the thoughts that you could be having, such as, *I wonder what's on TV tonight?*

(Always consult your doctor before starting a new diet or change in health plan. I am not a health practitioner or certified health consultant.)

Mud(dle) Through It

Sometimes it's just too big of a puddle to go around. You have to walk in it and through the slushy mess. Even if you're wearing your favorite shoes and prepared instead for rain with your umbrella.

It's a messy-life-puddle. There's good news, though. Once you're in it, once the shoes have already been dirtied, you have no reason to rush through it. Sometimes if you try to rush through it, you just make it messier. It then splatters on your favorite pair of jeans or your new white shorts. And I'll be the first to admit that you can get stuck in it. I've come out of it fully covered, unrecognizable, because I didn't know how to rinse it off. It can hold us back and deter us from our journey.

When we are kids, we want to play in the mud. But mom usually says, *"No…you'll get dirty!"* If you have lived even one day on this earth, one of the God-given gifts for you is that you will get dirty. Life isn't one big let's-stay-clean challenge.

As soon as we are born, there are already a few gazillion potholes laid out neatly waiting for us over the course of our lifetime. Even as we sit here reading, the universe is cultivating our next big challenge. So put on your big-girl panties and your "okay, here we go," attitude and don't worry. Just like breakfast and laundry are a part of our lives, so is mud.

The challenge isn't to get to the other side unmarred (where ever that might be for each of us), clean and utterly happy the whole way through. The challenge is what we will do once we get dirty while hurdling and trekking through it. Will we squish it through our fingers and hold it up to the light to see what it's made of? Will we just keep rinsing it away, as if that will be the end of it? Will we splash it off onto others around us making it an even bigger puddle?

It's not a place to stay long. We only have to travel through it. But if we don't take the lesson from it, we will come across that same mud puddle again and again until we've been able to navigate its murky depths thoroughly.

There's a reason for it, and even if we don't figure out its reason, it really is about how we handle ourselves through it. It's easy to be happy and pleasant when life is leading us through the paved route, but harder to keep a positive mind frame when traversing through the mud.

So imagine yourself sitting in the muck, dirty and upset and with no one close enough to pull you out. What do you do? Find a way to start with laughter. The first image you may have conjured up was of you sitting in the mud with a furrowed brow and muddy clothes. Now try looking at yourself sitting there in the same clothes, in the same spot, but this time smiling. Turn it into fun.

We first have to let go of how it has just interrupted our day (and our life). We have to change our plan at that very moment while sitting in it. We can't waste time and worry mourning about landing in it and what we were supposed to be doing instead. Because what we were supposed to be doing, is exactly that moment of change. It is opening your doorway to growth in some way that is a mystery. The old plan no longer exists. Make a new plan. Take extra time if you need it. Laugh through it somehow. Take photos!

There are mud puddles that I've been through and looking back on them now, their memories still don't bring any traces of a smile to my face when thinking about them. Yesterday's date marked the 17th anniversary of my miscarriage. I keep the date marked on my calendar because I always want to remember there was a baby. It doesn't make me smile but it doesn't make me sad, either. It makes me wonder about the possibility of having a sixteen-year-old in my life right now and how different life would be. It's not something to forget. But while I traveled that muddy road 17 years ago, I know that I smiled often between the tears.

We will get through our mud puddles, but we decide how. There will be an end to it. Find the faith that it's there for a reason and that there is a silver lining to it. Label your mud and yourself while there. Become a pro-mud wrestler in your Life Swamp, or a silver lining detective in your Murky Mystery. And guess what? You get to stomp through it sometimes, too. (Be a soldier on the A-(ha)-Team.)

So the next time your little one wants to stomp through a rain or mud puddle, don't tell him *no*. Tell him to go right ahead, and stand back and watch him smile.

Seven Days, on

Purpose

(This is my first blog ever published, January 2013. All of my stories come from my blog that is supportive to women and their lives. They were created one story at a time during my events and journeying. There are so many more to come!)

I LOVE Friday's. My favorite part has to be not having to set my alarm when I go to sleep that night. TOnight. (insert smiley face HERE.) So…Happy Friday, no matter what day you read this!

I decided to make my first blog about appreciation. There is so much

we expect from the world, but we seem to expect so much more

from ourselves. But if we were to imagine extending our arms

outward, we could fill up the empty space in front of us easily with

our abundance.

The fact that you can read my blog with healthy eyes, a computer or

a smartphone and an education all prove to be blessings. These items

are not needs, or something everyone has. We could also fill the

space with clean water, enough clothes and shoes (to dress a small

city's population, in my case), possibly a car to get us to where we

want to go, some of us have healthy children, our good friends and

family and lots and lots of food in the fridge and pantry. And let's

not forget the countless phone calls from mom, for some of us.

As women, we have *so* much work to do. So many things need our

attention on a daily basis. We all know how many times we go to bed thinking about the things that we didn't finish or what we could have done better. But it's important to remember and focus on the things that we did finish and did get right.

I recently attended a worship service (something I don't do enough). The lesson began as a reminder to be appreciative. There are seven days in a week, on purpose. The six days allow us to work and move forward and prosper and accomplish. The seventh day? It's time to stop to breathe it all in. For us to take a breath and then blow it all out. Even if you are working that day.

The seventh day allows us the time to think about all that we have done during the past week. What we have learned from it, and then the ability to wipe the slate clean. To forget and put aside the things that didn't get done. The people we didn't visit. The forgotten errands. Even if it was a hard week, we can find something good. Appreciate that you were able to get through it and that you're still here to celebrate it. Use it to rest and mentally prepare for the next week.

My day of thanks is Sunday, but it can be any day of the week. Just make sure that you have an ending and starting point somewhere in your week. Don't wait for special occasions to feel special. Your week *was* special.

This Is Me

("My Messy Beautiful")

How is it that the people with the cleanest homes are always the ones that say, *"Please excuse my messy house…I haven't had a chance to clean."?* They say it without embarrassment and I'm thinking with a bit of smugness hiding in their words. *"Trust me,"* I say, *"I know messy. There's no messy here."*

I am writing this essay-blog for the Messy, Beautiful Glennon Lloyd-Melton Project. (She wrote, Carry On Warrior.) And when you mention "messy" to me, the first thing I think of is my home.

Shouldn't it be a warm safe harbor, our home? I have days, a few

days of the year, where it feels that way. But there are *so* many days

where it is the enemy. A battle waiting to be won. Laundry should be

called "*laun*" because then it would be a four-letter word. And the

kitchen "*sink*" already is one. When my family and I aren't home

making a mess, I have a dog, a hamster (their urine really

stinks…don't get one…no one ever told me that) and Beta fish who

continue to do that while I'm gone.

I love coming home to a pretty home. When everything is in order

and there is nothing for me to work on the minute I walk in the door.

I LOVE pretty. I even put on some pretty text to sit down and write.

I've been through the real messy stuff, too. A miscarriage, a divorce,

the loss of my mom and then my dad a month later, (cancers…how

cruel) but I tend to not think of those things as messy. I don't write too much about them. They are all dear to my heart and so very sacred, but they don't make me different or lonely or in need of sympathy. They don't even make me messy. They make me normal. When I had the miscarriage, I felt awful. But on the same day as my D&C, I learned that one in three pregnancies end in a miscarriage. I suddenly felt normal. I had team members in large numbers by my side.

I like to keep things private to keep them less messy. When I had the miscarriage, no one even knew we were pregnant until the miscarriage. So no one else had the opportunity to mourn with me. A family friend dropped by after I came home from the procedure and wanted to say Hi. I said, *"I'm sorry…I'm not really up for company. I just had a D&C due to a miscarriage."* That was a messy moment. And *realllly* awkward. Only because I *realllly* didn't feel like talking.

My messy is me. I'm way too private. Except for when I'm behind my keyboard. I don't share enough about myself to really close friends. *("Oh, by the way, four years ago my husband had an affair and I'm still not dealing with it very well. Can we talk? Yes…that IS my secret diet and the reason why I'm way thin.")*

I find that if I talk about those messy matters, then I feel them way more often than I care to…or want to. They won't go away just because I'm feeling them more. I will still have to deal with them. But if I keep them private, I won't have to hear people say: *"how are you doing…are you okay?"* Because that's a reminder. A reminder of something that I would rather put aside until I'm alone and have the quiet space I need to try to figure out how I am going to embrace my new life. My life without that baby. A life as a single woman. That life without parents…without M.O.M.

O.M.G. Without Mom. Moms are everything. You don't know that until yours is gone. They are your foundation to every single living cell in your Being. Literally and figuratively.

So what is my messy-beautiful? I use this to pay tribute to my messy, beautiful mom. She was a pack-rat, so she knows a bit about a messy house. I'm sure that's where my messy house comes from. So it's not so messy, then. When you find those reminders of a Love that is gone, you inhale anything that reminds you of them. My sense of direction. I *love* getting lost on road trips. It reminds me of my mom and her bad sense of direction. My thighs, as much as they aren't so pretty, they remind me of my mom each time I look down and there she is. Mom lives on in me. And it can be messy, but I will never find myself apologizing for it. I will embrace it. Because I can no longer embrace her. Mom…you were Messy, but you were so Beautiful. I Miss You.

three

happy kids

Home Feat Home

It's true what they say; if your child behaves perfectly with others
(teachers, babysitters, friends), and then acts out with you, it means
that you are doing something right.

Your young one is smart enough to know what is expected of them
in life when they are out in the world (way to go, mom and dad!),
and they are smart enough to know that when they are home, they
are in a safety zone with their parents. Enough so that they can act
out without embarrassment or shame. It's called unconditional love.
We will love our children no matter what they do, and they know
this because we have made it clear to them.

They know that they are loved, even when they don't behave, even when they temper tantrum. We continue to want more of their sweet hugs and wet kisses. We are "home" to them. We are *safety*. Even if there is judgment at home, it is not detrimental to their survival or to their safe haven. We are going to be there for them. They are smart enough to know this, too. They can be who they are at their worst.

After they give away every ounce of their best behavior to the world, and the world in turn makes them feel insignificant, less than worthy or incompetent, they know that when they get back home, they can release all of the negative feelings that they have experienced into the safe hidden crevices of a home that is made up of hugs and unconditional acceptance. So they do.

That temper tantrum last night? That was from the previous days' experience of not getting a fair turn on the playground. And that break down last night right before bed? That was because they were ostracized by a group of close friends for a simple embarrassing mistake.

But we don't get to hear about the experiences. We only get to feel them. Their frustrations come barreling at us like a James-and-the-Giant-Peach-rhino-nightmare. They don't hold anything back. They let it all go until the steam and the pressure have been released into the air around us.

We need to be ready to stand to the side so that the heat doesn't scald us, but we also need to keep our hand on their shoulder to steady them. To remind them that we'll hold them up if they need us to, while they spew the bitterness of the world onto our lap.

We don't even need to know what problems they may have had. We just need to recognize that they had a problem that needs to be released, and then allow them the space and the time to do so.

So often a child's behavior is just a phase that will pass. But this behavior children have of acting out at home never goes away. We hold onto it throughout adulthood. We let loose on our loved ones.

We come home and guess who gets our bad mood? Our frustrations are served up on a platter to those who are home when we arrive. We get anxious and angry with the ones who are in front of us when we are running late. They feel our frustrations of life. Meanwhile, the people that we work with and play with and visit with see our softer, better behaved side. We are polite and politically correct. We don't trust them completely. Not like our home bodies.

Our home bodies will hopefully love us and our faults and mood distortions and anxieties and short tempers unconditionally. When our angst settles, they will know it and they will come up and give us that hug that the world never can. We can melt and falter and tear up, and they will glue us back together with only a few words that will comfort us and put us back on track to the person that we were minutes before. We need our 90 seconds of releasing our suffering and we need to be accepted while we do it.

The next time that you feel the anxiety from your little or big loved one, whether they are two or seventy-two, comfort them through it. Be strong for them when they can't be.

If temper tantrums happen at your house, you are safety. You are trusted. And you are unconditional.

I Raised My Son

My Daughter Raises Her

Eyebrows

My son and daughter are 10 years apart. The long pause was not the way I intended it, but it's the way nature intended. My son was conceived as soon as we began trying. Eazy-peezy. His dad and I dated and then became engaged. We were engaged forever. When we married, we planned to wait one year and then we would try for a baby. One year after our marriage, we were pregnant, as planned. Nice, neat and perfect. Besides the three-straight-months of 24/7 seasick nausea, everything went as planned. Even the drug-free delivery.

I didn't want to know whether we were having a boy or a girl. He did. So we decided that the ultrasound nurse would tell only him what we were having, and he swore himself to secrecy. We even did THAT perfectly. I was surprised when my son was born and he had the bris (circumcision celebration 8 days after birth for Jewish boys) all planned out, secretly and perfectly.

Then lots of love and happiness. My youthfulness and my firstborn made me more anal than ever. My son knew his alphabet and numbers and colors way too soon. He was a way too well-behaved-two-year-old. He wore perfect outfits. He took perfectly timed naps. He took baths at the perfect time so that dinner was always on the table at the perfect time. He went to bed at 6:00 p.m. and woke up perfectly at 6:00 a.m. And no, there was no crying himself to sleep at bedtime. I was there when and if needed, to help him slumber off peacefully and perfectly, without a tear drop.

And now I can recognize first time parents from a mile away. Only because I have had a second one. As my firstborn grew, I was pre-op in motion.

Me talking to my young son: *We need to get ready in ten minutes because it will take twenty minutes to get there. Make sure you've gathered whatever you want to take with you so that we can leave as soon as we need to.*

Him: *Okay.*

Me: *I packed a coloring book and crayons in case we have to wait awhile. I even put your special markers in there that you picked out at the store the other day.*

Him: *Okay.*

Me: *Go ahead and put your socks and shoes on now. That way we can really be ready.*

Him: *Okay.*

Me: *I'll go brush my teeth and then we'll be ready. Don't forget to brush yours.*

Him: *Okay.*

Me: *Is your seat-belt on? I can't pull out of the drive-way until you have it fastened tight.*

Him: *Okay.*

Me: *Are you cold back there? I have the air on too high. I'll turn it down a notch.*

Him: *Okay.*

Me: *I need to stop at the grocery store and get something really quick. We will just run in and out really quickly. No snacks or treats, okay?*

Him: *Okay.*

I don't know when it was that I realized how anal I was. I was always the one behind the camera at his birthday parties and our holidays. I think I heard myself talking during the videos when I'd replay them and I'd realize that I was over-thinking things (understatement). It was obvious in the audio.

I got better over time. The proof was on the videos; my silence. :)

In between my son and daughters' birth (ten years later), I got older in so many ways. Lots of messy things happened and helped age my brain and me. I don't record videos of my daughter as often as I did with my son (kind of a second, third, fourth child symptom of well-meaning parents), but I hear myself all the same. My brain is now more used and abused as my daughter grows up. I'm older, too.

Me talking to my daughter: *What time were we supposed to be there?*

Her: *Thirty minutes ago.*

Me: *Okay.*

Me: *Did we buy the birthday gift yet?*

Her: *Yes. An iTunes gift card.*

Me: *Okay.*

Her: *We need to stop at the store and pick up a birthday card still.*

Me: *Okay.*

Me: *Did you bring the invite? I need the address.*

Her: *Yes. I put it in your purse.*

Me: *Okay.*

Me: *Is it a sleepover?*

Her: *No. Pick me up at 3:00.*

Me: *Okay.*

I can look at my two kids, now 21 and 11. My son, he makes me a walking smile whenever I'm around him. He's made choices already in his life that have put him on a path that his mom and dad can be proud of. He shines with wit and love and grace. He made it through completely; all that coddling and doting and perfectionism and helicoptering-mom. He's wonderfully independent and polite and confident and knowledgeable. And he made it to adulthood beautifully.

One word to describe him. This is the first time I have tried to define him in one word. It's gotta' be good. *Bright!* Both literally and figuratively. I have succeeded as a mom, even with all that overprotective sticky stuff.

My daughter, being 11, is beginning middle school. I love that she doesn't fret the cool quota. She could care less about being "cool," which in my mind makes her way cool. She wants to be "her" no matter who everyone else thinks she should be. She's on her own path. She adheres to my advice but always spouts her opinion when it doesn't match hers. You can't make her do something she doesn't want to do, but what she doesn't want to do is within reason. It's usually things I wouldn't want to do either.

One word for her? One wish she always had as a younger girl was to fly. She'd ask Santa every year to give her the ability to fly. Any water fountains that have my coins in it were wishes for flight. My word for her? *Flight!* She's gonna' fly as high or as low as SHE wants to. No one will control her direction. Not even me.

My kids; they had two very different mama's. I read in a book on birth order that each child of a family is born into a different family than their sibling before. Parents' mindsets change and attitudes soften over time. There are more family members each time. But I know that if we lace it with love on any day and every day, they will be fine. Even through our mistakes and through our experimental behavior as parents or lack of experience. They'll be fine as long as they know that love is full and forth coming and available day and night. As long as they know that they don't have to be perfect and that mom and dad will always love them and be there no matter what their mood is or what kind of day anyone has had. They will be okay. And the more human and genuine we are with ourselves around them, the more okay they will be. Okay?

21 Years as a Guide is

Plenty

"I have a son that is twenty-one."

Eight words that I have never said in one sentence until recently. It didn't sting. Kids are a Work-In-Progress. From the time that we find out that we are pregnant and begin eating healthier to prepare them for a sustainable life, we concentrate on keeping them well until the day that we die.

My sister once told me that children are like precious raw stones. At first they have lots of rough edges but with beauty, lots of beauty hidden within. With our polishing and support and love, they will eventually shine and glisten and be beautiful inside and out, especially when put into the light. It's the same sister that became very frustrated and sad when her daughter didn't want to see her dating after her divorce. She was an adolescent and wanted/needed to have her mom available to her, not off gallivanting with another person foreign to her. So then it was my turn to give her the advice.

"You know how you have to remind your daughter to brush her teeth Every. Single. Morning. And Every. Single. Night? Even though she knows she's supposed to and she can't leave the house without doing it?" (Think about it. How many times do you think you've said, "Go brush your teeth," as a parent?)

"Now, rinse and repeat this a hundred times, too, if you have to: I'm a mother first. And I'm a woman. And a woman deserves a companion in her life. It will be a slow process but eventually we will have another person in our life. Because I want that."

It's a lot more serious than brushing teeth, but the message has to be relayed a few hundred times in order to move forward. For everyone. For any lesson.

The good news? We have 21 years to keep rinsing and repeating lessons. There is no need to rush lessons. Besides, they won't learn in a rush. They will learn like the tortoise. Slow and steady.

What is important is that we as parents keep planting the seeds. The seeds that they spit back out at us. The seeds that they don't want to swallow. The ones that have too hard of a shell for them to digest just yet. The seeds that sit there dormant. Until they remember them again. Until they *need* them.

And if we have forgotten to plant them, they won't ever have them to dig up and fertilize and grow all on their own. We can't rush a rose or a gemstone. And we can't try to rush them into adulthood.

Another idea to not rush them into. So many of us think of 21 (or 18)

as the "drinking age." And if we think of it as the "drinking age,"

guess what? So do our kids. There are religions that have rites of

passage to adulthood. Religion seems to have become unpopular but

we still need to keep an adult rite of passage alive.

When there is a bar mitzvah or bat mitzvah (a Jewish boy or girl,

respectively, turning 13 and 12), one of the reasons for celebrating is

their coming-of-age. They are now responsible for their own actions.

They should now think, act and practice responsibly. This is

something that they work towards their whole life. It's not just a

party. It's what children need in order to become productive human

beings and positive contributors to our society. We can't make the

age of 18 about, "*Then* and only then can you get a tattoo," or "Then

you can do whatever you want. Right now you're under *my* roof!"

We need to build them towards 18 (or 13 or 16 or 21) as a

responsibility. "You will join the world in helping it become a better

place!" "You will be ready to join the work force and find your passions." "You one day will find the love of your life and have beautiful children and make me a grandmother."

The United States borders Mexico. Mexico's drinking age is 18. We have many teenagers who cross over the border just so that they can drink freely and without worry. I remember a story years back where the U.S. was very upset with the effects of a lower drinking age and we felt that Mexican authorities should raise theirs in order to prevent the drinking, driving and accidents occurring when these children would drive back home across the border. Mexico's response?

Our children don't go out and party and drink until they are drunk the day that they become of drinking age. You need to talk to your kids about the responsibilities of drinking. Our drinking age isn't the problem.

We can't make drinking a "rite of passage" to adulthood. Because then our children will. It shouldn't even be a part of the equation.

I'm not even close to saying they shouldn't be drinking. I like my wine! And my son knows it. But he also knows that his mom has so many other priorities. And that's how he knows me and how he's come to know himself. He follows his heart, and I love that. Twenty-one years in the making, but I'll be honest, he was super special at any age. And that's what our kids need to know the most.

It Takes One to Grow One

Jody Foster has said that her mother used to tell her as a child to "always be kind." That doesn't mean you have to be friends with everyone. It means never be mean. Being kind is easy to do. Something else that is easy to do is *worry.* And also very relatable. Everyone does it, but how good are we at keeping it in the background versus the foreground? Especially once we have children. The first child born commences more than enough worry from both parents, but you come to find as time passes that all of your worrying wasn't necessary. Those horrible worries never transpired for many of us. You worry most about accidents and injury and health problems.

In your life before kids, a friend's child with a cold was just a child with a runny nose. Once you have your own child, a cold will surely turn into pneumonia or bronchitis. You'll check on them to make sure they are able to breathe through the night. You'll feel their chest to ensure it rises and falls with each breath. You'll feel their tiny head to make sure they are warm with life.

If they live through the first part of their life, you will then worry about what friends they will choose, what activities they will become involved in, how they behave in school, will they lie, steal, do drugs?

When my son was fourteen, he had asked me if he could see a movie that I felt he was too young for. He really wanted this but my answer was always no. In one of his last attempts at trying to convince me that I should trust him, he explained that it wasn't as if he was a drug-addicted teenager or binge drinker. And how I should be thankful for who he was. And I was. But I told him that he also had to think about who his parents were, and it contributed greatly to who he was. And that my decisions were always based on my concern and care for him. He lost the argument and didn't get to see the movie. But one year later, he had been talking with his friends about planning a trip to Busch Gardens that summer without parents.

He asked me if I would allow him to go if they all decided to do it. It took me only a few seconds.

I knew a normal response would be, *"no, you're too young."* But that was a normal response, and it would be cheating him of my genuine thoughts. I searched in my mind for reasons as to why he couldn't go and I couldn't think of any. So I simply said, *"yes."* It didn't take him any time at all to ask, *"Why!?"* Surely because he expected a "no." *"Because you've never given me any reason to say no."*

He and his friends didn't end up doing the trip that summer, but we both discovered in a simple moment that he was trusted in a very big way, making him and me very proud of him.

So look at yourself. Look at your spouse. Chances are good that your child will be just like you. Your habits. Your morals. Your personalities. So if you find yourself worrying that your child might one day become a convict, look at yourself first. Then realize that if you're not one, it's very unlikely that they will become one.

They truly don't fall far from the apple tree. If you are proud of the family that you are, it is safe to say that you will be proud of them. If you allow your husband to insult you and talk down to you, don't be surprised when your son will one day begin doing it.

They are learning as they are growing, including the age where they think that they know everything. If you always support them and never give up on them, they will know that they are worthier than what your worries amounted them to.

Worry is wasteful. Contemplation is fine. It helps you to consider problems that *may* arise and how you would handle them if they did. But worry is just stress dressed in a different dress. It gives you no enjoyment and no steps forward.

There's a Light at the End of the Tunnel. You.

So let your child make those steps forward. Don't worry about the falls and the hurts and the hurdles, because they are all supposed to happen. It's the kind thing to do. It will make them stronger.

Don't Pass on Passion.

Pass it on.

It was nearing Mother's Day and I really wanted to write a blog about my mom, but I'm finding I'm still selfish about her memory. Almost ten years have passed since she has. I'm pretty stingy. So I will write about passions instead. My mom had hers and in later years she was too busy with either work or her ten grandchildren (other passions of hers), to fully enjoy them, not that she ever voiced regret. Her greatest passion was, after family and friends, art. She painted, pasteled, sketched and drew. I knew her passion at a very young age. I remember when I was four or five years old watching my dad add his touches to one of her oil paintings that she had left out to dry. Like any child that age that was protective of their drawings, I was shocked that he'd paint on her work. I don't know what happened when she found out, but the memory that her art was sacred to her stayed with me. We should all know that about mom at a young age.

During the weeks leading up to Mother's Day, as a preschool teacher there are motherly projects that we work on each year. One is a questionnaire for our students asking them about their mom.

How old is your mom?

How much does she weigh?

What's her favorite color?

A lot of the children's answers are fun and they tend to reflect their feelings instead of their mom's. More questions:

What makes your mom laugh?

What would your mom do if she had more time?

What does your mom love to do to relax?

I love it when they have an immediate answer without having to think about it, no matter what their answer is. It means that they have seen the happiness on her face when she does the things that she loves. Even if it's sitting down to watch a favorite TV show or sleeping in.

I recently asked my daughter what she felt my passions were. She knew them.

"Writing, drawing, Haagen-Dazs Chocolate ice-cream and butterflies!"

I *was* surprised that she left out a few. I love putting on my pajamas, and I love getting into bed. She knows this for sure. Those aren't all of my passions, but I'd passed this mommy test.

Sometimes I have students who can't think of anything that makes their mom happy. Her passions are theirs. This is true for me as well. To see my daughter or my son have fun and smile and laugh is a passion beyond words. Even more so if they are doing it together. So yes, I love to see her ride her bike or dance in her recital and watch him play lacrosse with his team, but it's just as important for them to see *my* passions.

Instill passion in your children. Not by telling them to be passionate about their hobby, but by letting them see *your* passionate self. When you want to put on your pajamas, don't say, *"I'm going to put on my pajamas, I'm exhausted."* Instead say, *"I'm going to put on my pajamas. Who's with me!?"*

And argue a little bit harder when they want to eat your last bite of that chocolate ice-cream cone. *"You can have a couple of bites, but save the last one for me!"* Pass on the passion. Let them know that life is to be enjoyed, even the small things. Especially the small

things.

Grounding Your Kids the

Healthy Way

Summer has begun and my eyes are showing some signs of sleeping in. Waking up to crevices of the suns' light seeping in through the blinds is a peaceful way to wake up. It's exactly how nature intended it to be.

Waking in the dark has never made sense to my physical being. And the absence of the vibrating sound of my phone alarm in the darkness improves the start to my day ten-fold.

I love how the lighted summer mornings also allow me to see the wispy eyelash shadows on my daughters' cheeks as she sleeps in a quiet slumber that would normally be hidden in the dark on school mornings.

I love having peace in my life. It seems you need it even more when things aren't so peaceful.

My to-do list will keep me from solitude for a portion of the summer. It weaves itself slowly throughout the house from my bathroom to lanai, and my name is written all over it since I am the only adult that lives here. Let it be known that I will have a pretty little 11-year old helper.

I have two kids, but one is an adult. He is 21 and is still socially busy since before his pre-puberty days. I see him during summer breaks but never long enough to put him to work. He would if I asked but instead I cherish our rare visits together as talks and relaxing times. With only one child at home now, I don't have the sibling rivalry, but I have friends that are ready for summer to end and could easily send their kids back to school as we speak.

From past summers, I always found that "grounding" activities kept us more in sync and with more hair left on my head by summers end.

There are spiritual definitions of "grounding" but it also occurs easily with basic activities. Touching nature is one large accessible open-doorway to "grounding."

In my classroom as a preschool teacher, I keep play bins for my students on a counter for easy access. Sand is messy in a classroom, so instead I keep one bin filled with small gravel and another one filled with dried black-eyed peas, both with either scooping toys or small tractors. So very often a child will wander over to them and play quietly for long periods of time. You can witness the calm come over them as they play and interact with their classmates. Our hands touching nature is more magical than fun. It is peace inducing.

When the beginning of summer nears, putting these ten activities down on your to-do list will help keep you sane and keep your kids grounded. They are even better when the whole family does them together. Making memories while grounding doubles the benefits.

1)   Find a local farm and pick fruit. Touching nature at its best!

2)   Make sand castles in the yard or at the beach or park.

3)   Build with glue and popsicle sticks (wood). Let imagination
lead the way.

4)   Gather leaves from outside of all colors and create a collage
by gluing onto paper.

5)   Make snow cones. (ice = water)

6)   Make mud pies. Water and dirt equals major grounding!

7)   Find smooth stones in the yard or garden and make Pet
Rocks.

8)   Build a campfire. Don't worry that you might not be able to
light it. Pretend to make S'mores by using graham crackers,

marshmallow spread and a chocolate spread to make Indoor S'mores!

9)   Build a Domino maze (wood). Make it travel through the house even longer than my to-do list.

10)   Have everyone sketch (charcoal, lead or pencil) a picture of their own version of nature.

Gardening is also a great activity with the earth, seeds and water combination. Have a picnic on the lawn or even in the rain. Go swimming. And don't forget that most sports balls are made out of leather. When our children play ball, they are being grounded even then.

If you have an indoor day because you are tending to your to-do list and you have broken up the tenth argument of the day, drop everything and take them outside, including yourself. I remember many late nights when one of my babies wouldn't stop fussing and nothing could soothe them. When the stroller, the car ride or dancing to music didn't work, I'd finally come to my senses and just take them outside, even if it was three-o'-clock in the morning. They'd calm the instant the fresh air hit their tiny lungs. Never forget the resources that we have. The outdoors are available in unlimited amounts.

Most of these activities won't cost a cent and have many benefits of fun, grounding and surely lots of laughter by the time the fun is done. Your children will be calmer and more relaxed if you do it often.

Remember that when school is around the corner again, it comes with new teachers, new classes and possibly a new school, which will create a new stress for them. Continue with the grounding activities to help them come back to a peaceful state of mind. And make sure that you're close by to catch the conversations that will happen when they are happy and peaceful and inside of their young minds. The best conversations happen then, not when we are trying to pull information out of them on the ride home after a long busy day at school.

If time-outs and grounding for bad behavior happen at your house, the "grounding" activities are a good replacement to help children "pull themselves back together again." You won't have to discipline as often. Do them the favor, as well as yourself. Get dirty and enjoy. Happy Grounding!

four

healthy choices

Love Thy Selfie

I love my iPhone. I mean it. I *love* it. Before iPhones, there were iPods. Even then I wanted to kiss the feet of the inventor because I love music so much. He so knew what he was doing. Small pieces of pretty metal and wire and buttons with huge impacts on earth, history and on my life. The camera feature is the most adored. It simplifies selfies for our social media lifestyle generation. Is anyone even camera shy anymore?

My mom. She hated having her photo taken as much as I love my camera feature; passionately. When we decided to do a slide show for her memorial service, my three sisters and I ran in our four different directions to gather photos of her.

We all came back with many photos of my mom holding her hand up in front of her face, of her face turned sideways, downwards or looking uncomfortably away at someone standing out of the cameras' lens. Rarely did anyone capture the sparkle in her eye or the calming mood she cast on her family. She wanted to be in the background, not the foreground. And we let her.

My dad *was* a camera. I saw his Nikon more than I saw his face. When I look over his photos taken when we were children, it is obvious that he loved taking photos of my sisters and me. He told many stories of our lives with his film and slides. It's also obvious that he cherished us and our cute little noses and bright blue eyes. He captured them again and again (and again).

You hold memories longer when you can keep referring back to the photos that captured them. He has been gone ten whole years but his thoughts and emotions are revealed and brought to life each time I pull out his pictures.

I do wish he had turned his camera on my mom as often as he did on my sisters and me, but I have a feeling that she did the same with him, too. So, like me, he probably stopped trying to take her picture.

Photo images are so different from our reflection in the mirror. In a mirror you can convince yourself that what you see isn't what everyone else sees; the spots, the muffin top, wrinkles, the age, the extra weight.

But when you look at a photo, the evidence is clear and permanent and obvious. I am not at all photogenic, but even so, I'll see my photo someone took of me and think, *my hair LOOKED okay when I left the house that day,* or, *I looked fine in the mirror at home. What happened after?* Maybe it's what makes us so intrigued by our own photo. I have a brother-in-law who has used a wheelchair since he was a young adult. He told me that when he sees his photo, it's hard to take in what he sees; himself in a wheelchair.

Seeing ourselves in a photo forces us to see who we are to the outside world. To people who don't know us and to people who do. I think that someone really nice must have made up that lie about the camera instantly adding on ten pounds. Dare I say, maybe it's what we actually look like? Maybe we don't like what we see so we sugar coat it.

There was a time when I used to have my photos developed. (Ha.) I had left a stack of new photos on the kitchen counter in my to-do pile waiting to be put into my photo album. My then husband kept putting a specific photo of me on top of the stack. I'd come home later and see it there and I'd hide it back under the rest of the photos. The next day, it would be back on top of the pile. It went on for a few days until I finally asked him why he kept moving it to the top. *"It's a beautiful picture of you. I like to look at it."* I went back to the photo to look for the beauty or even a trace of pretty. I didn't see it. I saw the meaty thigh and the messy hair and the nervous smile. I didn't look at myself differently after that. I looked at him differently. He had a much softer eye than I did and I wanted his view.

I imagined that he must view me in the same way that I view my kids; beauty no matter what angle I'm watching them from. It doesn't matter what they are wearing or if they've brushed their hair. If they had ice-cream cone remnants dripping from their face, they were even more beautiful. They're at their most beautiful while they sleep, when I can peek in on them in the sunlit mornings with their delicate resting innocent features so bare and pure.

I took a lot more photos of my firstborn than my second, but now with my second born, I carry around a phone with a built-in camera. The chances of me taking her photo have gone way up. She is beautiful to me and I often take her photo when she isn't paying attention. And I can look at her photo again and again and the beauty is always there. Why can't I do that with myself?

Maybe we'll all become more and more comfortable with our own photos because of the accessibility. Because of our selfies.

If my mom were alive, I could be holding my phone in front of me and be taking her picture without her knowing it. I could have recorded her beautiful innocence and peace.

We carry our phones with us everywhere. Treasure and use your camera often. Take as many selfies as you want. Learn to love what you see. And take more Momsies for me. And make sure that you tell her how beautiful she is when she looks at her image in disgust. It's hard to watch ourselves age, and it's no different for moms. Fight her on this one and don't let her win. Kiss her feet, if you have to. She's worth it.

Label Your Day

I conquered the grocery store the other day. I put my labeling technique to use. I was pushing my empty cart up and down the aisles. I wasn't even hungry, thank goodness. We all know you can't go there when hungry. I'm trying to drink less soda because I drink too much of it. I had no more in the house. So, when I came upon the soda aisle, I looked my trusty diet cola friend in the eye and labeled him, "poison" and just walked on by. Strength in action!

Next was the cereal aisle. My inner voice called down the aisle, "gluten!" and I kept on walking. Next challenge? My red wine. I love my red wine but it has a new name. "Bad. For. My. Skin." It was at this moment that I had that *"how proud am I?"* feeling.

Have you ever noticed that the displays at the ends of the aisles are the worst? I have no problem seeing those powdered sugar donuts, unless they are in my pantry, and the double-stuffed sandwich cookies aren't my favorite, but there's still some things that are on my "gotta have it" list. I was pretending I was having to give up something, so I was trying to give up everything and that usually back fires on me, but on this day I was puffing-my-chest-proud. I did pick up chocolate, though. The only label I could think of was "addiction."

So labeling works! What about Labeling Your Day? When you wake up in the morning, if you are anything like me, you know what needs the most attention that day, besides work, children and always laundry. Before your head is off of your pillow and your feet hit the floor, label your day with the items that you want to get done that day. I'm happy to report that today I got it all done. And that never happens. I labeled my day first thing this morning "accomplishment." I had written a list in the kitchen that I'd see while preparing breakfast so that I'd know what that was going to entail.

You may have days where you just want to fly by the seat of your pants. I highly recommend labeling it instead, even if it's to label your day as "play day, relax day or peaceful day."

Maybe you have drawers that have been calling your name out for days or weeks! Clean and organize them but first label your day "organize." Organize the drawers, emails, digital photos on the computer (including saving them to another form of back-up…we all know why). Plan for laundry day, errand day, pet care day (baths, toenails clipped).

We all have a constant streaming to-do list running through our heads of things needing immediate attention. What is *the* one thing (or two) that you'd love to have done by the end of your day? Label your day as such.

When you label your day first thing, you will feel more motivated and have a sense of direction instantly. And once those items are taken care of and you meet yourself back at your pillow again later that night, you will feel accomplished. That's a pleasant feeling at

the end of a day. Even if the house is still a mess and you forgot to

schedule dental appointments once again, your goal has been met.

Success! Make your day conquerable. And then go conquer it.

Destination Known

It's summer and I haven't headed anywhere yet. As a preschool teacher, I'm home for the summer with my son and daughter. I like to decompress in the first part of summer but today I've realized that after three full weeks of summer passing, I haven't started doing that yet. I'm still floundering in the To-Do's. I've gotten a lot done but I haven't completed projects that I wanted to have finished by now. In fact, I've even started new ones that could have waited until later. I'm floundering.

We all know where we are going. Most of us can safely conclude it's upwards.

And I'm not talking about where we are going tomorrow, where we are going next week or where we are going next year. I mean, where we are GOING, going. So while we are down here, we need to make sure that our days lead upwards.

The destination we are inevitably heading towards doesn't need to be on our minds every day, but our direction should be.

Not many people know it, but we have an imaginary ladder that sits outside of our front door every day. It's there for climbing and descending. Our ladder helps us to know where we are. When we leave the house, will we be one rung higher when we return home or one lower? One rung upwards constitutes feeling good about yourself and making others feel good during our time out that day. If we came home feeling remorseful about how we made someone feel today, or if we made bad decisions while at work, our ladder *and* our spirit are getting rung down. Yes, traffic was bad, but we made it home safely. Worry about the ladder, not the traffic. Our days affect us all inwardly. How we handle it will then determine the rest of our day, and probably the rest of our family's day, too. So when we put our key in our door or pull into our garage, we should check the ladder.

We can vow to be Rung Leaders. Our rungs are endless so we can go

as high as we want to. It's the one place not to be afraid of heights.

As Rung Leaders, we get extra distance if we allow others to climb

up our ladder with us. Give a rung away once in a while and believe

it or not, you'll gain more rungs.

It's easy to earn rungs. You don't have to come home with a big

paycheck, a new car or even organic groceries. It's three (3) simple

things: you just need to be kind, thoughtful and world embracing.

What should we do today to help us finish one rung higher,

minimum, by days end? Just be kind and you'll become a Rung

Leader with lots of followers. It's not possible to go past the top rung

no matter how hard we try. There are always more rungs. But it does

count later. LATER, later.

So I'll continue working on my To-Do's and my stock pile of

paperwork and on my floundering. But when we reach our final destination, we won't be looking back down the ladder at our To-

Do's and workload and cars and houses and furniture. We will look

back at our leadership, our actions, our children and how we affected

others. No one up there is going to say, but your

laundry…gosh…you never once completely finished it. They will

notice how many people were able to use your ladder and how they

will be using it for years to come. And you will be crowned a Rung

Leader. If you want to head in that direction, put your kind,

thoughtful, embracing crown on now, and you'll never have to worry

about whether it's going to fit or not. It just will.

W.W.C.D?

(What Would Cavemen Do?)

I don't remember where I was headed. Maybe taking my daughter to dance class? Where ever it was, I wanted to first stop at Starbucks for gas. (smile) I've recently traded my dear friend diet cola for a newer, friendlier gas; iced-chai tea latte (yum). On my way in that direction, I wondered what the cavemen did when they were running low. (I'm odd that way.) My guess is that they lied down on the closest flat boulder in the warm sun with the breeze blowing on their sweaty skin, and went to sleep. (I must have *really* been tired.) They didn't have to worry about traffic or the grocery store errands or dance class or volleyball or soccer or being late for meetings. Their sports were of course catching food. No grocery carts for them.

I know what you're thinking. Dinosaur danger. I think we also have dinosaurs. Much bigger ones. Too much television, cellphones, electronics, violent movies and video games, bullies, alcohol, cigarettes, drugs, sugar…flour.

The worst thing is that we allow our dinosaurs to lie down next to us and chill. We pet them and give them names.

I'm not being judgmental. I LOVE sugar, flour, wine and The Blacklist (TV). My iPhone is more dear to me than any other item in my purse. Remember when wallets were special? RIGHT NOW AS WE SPEAK, my daughter is watching a Mine Craft video on her iPad. That is allowing me the time to write this. (Smile, again.)

I imagine cavemen didn't try to keep up with the Jones's, either. *My cave is better than your cave.* No…I imagine it was more like: *your cave has a brontosaurus in it? Bring your tribe on over. We're having a non-barbecue tonight of slaughtered pterodactyl. B.Y.O.U.* (Bring your own utensils.)

It's hard to imagine which life is a simpler life. You know how I am about worry. Being cavewomen, we would have a very different worry world. But worry is worry and it would still inhibit our muscular bodies and simple minds. It's a female habit.

The world was cleaner then. Skies, soil, oceans. Will we ever be able to undo all the done? Is there anyone that can make things the way that they were? Or is it the universe that decides? *"Okay. You guys are getting carried away aGAIN! But THIS time, you get a choice:*

Do you prefer a flood, terrorists, or food poisoning? A flood is rather quick, terrorism is very violent, or do you just want to keep eating the way you do from the land that you poison? That one takes a long time. Lots of suffering. Strictly your choice."

Maybe we could make a deal with it. What if we started cleaning? If we all knew that we would have to start over, would we all work together? Would we stop the senseless crimes and bullying and earth destruction? There's a *lot* of people here that would have to agree with one another. If we *knew* that we had to fix it in order to survive, of course we would start right away, wouldn't we?

Where do cavemen go when they want to feel safe? That's what we could start with. If we start with our homes and work outwards, we could save ourselves from the dinosaurs. Maybe we could eventually stop using so much gas so that they didn't have to die in vain! We could just walk to Starbucks, instead.

And I realize that dinosaurs were in a different era than the cavemen, but that makes me wish that our dinosaurs were as well.

Don't Forget to take out

the Garbage

I spend more time than I care to admit on my social websites. And if you asked me to give them up, my whining would begin; *"but it's fuuuunnnn..."* And it is. I think a lot of it has to do with my love of reading and my love of writing. I get to do both here. And I'm learning, too. I've also been inspired more times than I can count, and Pinterest seems like the most beautiful virtual place to vacation. I always sign-off inspired! I've done nothing, but I've felt something.

A little like the feeling that we might get at church or temple. You've sat through the sermon doing nothing, and then you come away with something. Something that wasn't there when you sat down.

I know we've all sat at tables in restaurants and watched half of the diners peering into their phones or devices while eating together. It appears that we've checked out from socializing, even with family at times. But I have to admit that I love it when people are sharing their finds with the people around them. There have been countless fits of the giggles that I've witnessed as they hold up their phone to those next to them with shock and laughter on their faces. We have become very religious about our social networks. And we can complain or click our tongues at it all that we want, but it's here to stay. (I hope!) We can also embrace it.

My own keep-in-touch-with-friends-and-family ratio has gone way up. In the past, I've kept in touch with family and friends that have moved away with my annual holiday newsletter. Once. A. Year. While receiving their years' worth of news in the same way or in a neatly written Christmas card with good wishes.

Now? I get to see and hear about their holidays and vacations and kids' birthday parties and job accomplishments and weekend activities and what they had for dinner and what movie they saw (with their review!) and what animal crawled in through their doggie door last night, as it happens(!) with their photos and status updates! Even if I only comment, "Looks like a fun day!" I'm saying more than what I would have said to them during the whole year through. So, YESWAY, I'm quite happy with my social media obsession.

I often "friend" or "join" other social user's pages that seem inspiring or fun. If we are going to be so religious about our social networking, we might as well make it like church. Make sure it's inspiring, fun and a positive influence on our lives. Let it move us forward in life, not weigh us down with *more* bad news, bad relations or bad karma. I don't watch the news on TV. I get email updates from news organizations to get the highlights, but when I sit down and *try* to watch the news (because I feel like I really should), by the third story, I have to turn it off. Especially if my daughter is sitting close by. It's depressing. Plugging in only positive influences into our day is a better way.

The written word is powerful. It's why I can't make myself throw away those twenty-five women's magazines that I've yet to read. They're full of WORDS! But we can't let it be more powerful than us. Don't feel guilty about being addicted, but make rules. Not just for our kids. For ourselves, too. No social sites until the dishes are done. Or visit while dinner is cooking. Set a timer, though, if you don't like burned pot-roast. Promise yourself you'll get three things done around the house first before you get to sit down and troll. Allow yourself only laptop or desktop computer time for social media and save your phone for checking emails only. I know that *my* emails are adding up. Probably because my Facebook page is so much more fun. Does anyone else have "255 unread emails?" Be honest.

So do plug-in certain times of the day. Make your social networking the "later," not the necessities. And treat your pages religiously. Stop "friending" or "following" anything or anyone that isn't a positive influence on your day. Don't let another's negativity bleed into your day. At least not voluntarily. That's Garbage-In, Garbage-Out.

There's a Light at the End of the Tunnel. You.

Dispose and Delete. Promise yourself positive posts only. Good-in, Good-out. And recycle the best ones by sharing. Happy Socializing!

five

unjudging

pro-choice but anti-abortion

I saw a bumper sticker the other day that was supportive of anti-abortion. I always find these stickers bordering on the quite-offensive. To anybody, no matter what your belief. Too many graphic images and successful efforts of inducing disturbing thoughts. I know this is on purpose. We want to save another sweet life.

But. If we are sending messages out to the world for good, shouldn't we be making sure that it's conducive to spreading Knowledge, Truth AND Peace? I know the authors of these stickers are diligently trying to make a difference in our world by saving one more baby. I give thanks for that. But no one says that they have to be mean about it.

The bumper sticker I saw the other day was Kind. Thoughtful. And Decent. And of course I can't remember it, but it said something to the effect of, *"Don't let me go. Hold my hand instead, "* with an image of a tiny newborn. These are words a sweet soul might whisper into her mother's ear during that difficult time of decision making. That made sense. I didn't take offense.

I could not choose abortion, but I've never been in a position to have to choose. I also feel very strongly that the government has no business deciding a woman's extremely personal decision for her. If abortion was illegal, we know that women all over the world would still find a way to abort it if she really wanted to. It wouldn't stop it from happening.

I don't think it's up to us to make her feel bad about her decision, either. I'm pretty sure she feels bad already. Remember the "no judging" clause? So I refuse to judge a woman on her decisions. I would definitely feel like judging whoever invented the idea of abortion. I can only imagine the public outcry when it first emerged.

An unwanted pregnancy can definitely be a negative, for many. But adoption would turn it into making sense, for everyone. It could be turned into a positive. First, by not aborting and second by giving a family a child they've been waiting on for more than the brief nine months that it takes to carry one. Either way, this decision is going to be so hard for any woman, but something very good can come out of it if the baby is saved.

1) Someone will gain a cute little family member.

2) The biological mom will have the opportunity in about 18 years, to meet their kindred little one, all grown up and wondering about her, too.

3) You get to keep your Choice; yours. Will I one day see my child, or won't I?

When a baby is adopted out, the birth mother has more and more say-so over how they want to hand over their child.

"I want contact. I don't want contact. I want to know their name. I want to know where they live. I don't. I want to be able to get in touch with them when they are of age. I don't."

Don't sever choices. If a child is aborted, all of those future choices will disappear with the baby.

Yes, we want fewer abortions in the world. But keep the government and the cruel thoughts out of it. Keep the Kindness in all of our decisions. Kindness towards girls and woman with difficult decisions. Kindness towards a child that was meant to be. Kindness used to spread kindness.

UnTainting Color

The controversy and racial tensions over the Ferguson city police shooting of Michael Brown took over our emotions for days and days. We weren't there and can't judge or decide what happened that night, but most of us have witnessed racial discrimination. It is born and reborn. It can't be snuffed out as long as it exists in even the smallest of amounts.

The color of our skin shouldn't make a difference any more than the color of our car does. I won't judge someone for having a blue car just because I have a white car. We are born into our skin and it serves the same purpose for everyone; to keep us healthy and to protect us.

So why then, does the color sometimes hold someone back, limit them and hurt them in some way? Why, for so many people, can they not look past someone's skin and instead look into their eyes to see them?

I worked as a cashier at a local grocery store during my high school years. One of the bag boys that was African-American often bagged groceries for me at my counter. He was teenager-shy enough that I never got to know him but he was always quiet and kind to customers and co-workers.

A family known only by sight shopped at our store often. In my line one day, their soggy-diapered almost two-year old son sat in their cart behind me as I checked out their groceries. Half way through their order I heard his tiny scratchy voice yell the "N" word out in anger, and when I turned, he was pointing at my bag boy with his barely two-year-old disgust and accusatory stare. It was loud enough to draw the stares of the employees and customers at the front of the store, not towards his target, but at his parents standing in front of me. Everyone silently piqued a need for their reaction.

They yelled at their son to quiet down. His confident anger dwindled into his pale, mosquito-bitten skin as he dropped onto his swollen diaper, hidden now within the large section of the cart. He was immediately a toddler again. The parents stood closer to one another in discomfort and unity. There was no apology for the employee. Only flushed skin, dirty hair and two smirks.

The stares followed the family out the glass doors. I heard the sounds of solemn mumbles among everyone while I stood nearest to my bag boy, his head down while preparing more doubled paper bags for our next order, his skin not showing red embarrassment under the darker tones.

"Someone had to teach him that," escaped from my teenage lips. "I know," he said, with an air of having had it happen before.

They were that "smallest of amount" of racism. Someone that believed that color was to be judged.

A two-year-old hating before he could even understand hate. It was ugly. Two-year-olds are supposed to be cute and lovable and mischievous, which he went right back to being when he sat down.

He was oblivious to the discussions he'd perpetrated, the emotions felt, the unity of a crowd it created, the memory that carried forward even decades later.

I have no memory of the bag boy after that day. I can't remember if that was his last day or if he continued working there. But I can still see his grace and peace behind me getting ready for the next customer. I pulled from it and moved forward, too. I let it go as they left our parking lot.

They continued to return to our store, now with the void of any grace or class or dignity. A tainted memory of low-class behavior and my thoughts of their son's angry future that was well on its path.

Who would he meet one day that might change his mind and undo the anger and hatred? There was an opportunity for it to change that day if the parents had only watched and witnessed how ugly it was. How is it that they saw color as something uglier than their behavior?

The parents of Michael Brown asked for peace to return to their city after the rioting and looting began. A city swimming in bitterness was not going to help anyone. I saw no bitterness around me in the grocery store that day. I saw disgust and shock and then quiet and dignity. Everyone kept calm instead of adding their anger. But everyone there that day felt the moment and took it home with them.

It's Time

It keeps happening. This dog of mine. I cleaned up his mess two times yesterday and once today. He knows to run and hide. I love this dog, but…

Ten years ago, I was finished with dogs as far as I knew. My little sweet part-Yorkshire-part-Chihuahua-part-Human mix, Beau, lived for seventeen years, thank you, God. He was my lovey little guy. He was my baby before I had babies. He was my dependence during my independence of living on my own. My mom decided (thankfully) that it would be wonderful for me to have a puppy in my new home. I was the last of four daughters to move out and I think she wanted to make sure that I wasn't lonely. I didn't even say the word and she was out looking. She found Beau at the Humane Society. She sold me on him even before I went to see him at the shelter. And OMG she was so right. Not necessarily the cutest little puppy ever and by no means ugly, but his personality shined so bright. How on earth

was he the last taken of a litter of four? They must have all had the

light. He was happy whether I picked him or not. He was playing

with some un-toy in his cage, looking me over and smiling, then

back to his un-toy. He had me at play. My little guy.

Over the years, I watched as friends' dogs passed away and were put

to sleep. Putting to sleep, I always said, I could never do that. When

he goes, he goes on his own. I can't make the choice for him. Until

that day seventeen years later. Until he could no longer eat because

of the tumor on the roof of his mouth, the sadness in his eyes that

showed more than the cataracts, the hunger over the food that he

wanted but gave him pain instead of satiation. It was after 10:00 p.m.

and we came home, my family of four, after a late night of visiting

and we saw it in his eyes. Time. It was time. He couldn't move. We

took him to the emergency animal clinic, not because we decided to,

but because no one could speak and we knew we had to do

something. The four of us drove silently towards the veterinarian's

needle. I was holding his quiet weak body but I don't remember the ride.

Months before, we'd learned that he had cancer and his doctor had told us that we should have mercy by not putting his seventeen-year-old blind, deaf, arthritic body through chemotherapy and surgery. Now there at the clinic, through my tight lips and wet eyes I could only say, "It's time," to the stranger who kindly looked us over to decide if he should argue it or not, not knowing my dogs' history. My eleven-year-old son was quiet. My one-year-old daughter was too young to know what was about to happen. Their dad holding her while I snuggled Beau taking the needle. He left a small hollow in my heart with his last breath. It wasn't easy, but it felt right.

At seventeen-years-old, he had his weaknesses. Cleaning up after him was not unusual, but until the end he always avoided carpets, the sweet little guy. So thinking about another dog was not in my future. Beau was irreplaceable and I wasn't interested in cleaning up after a potty-training new puppy, either.

Fast forward to almost two years later. Say "I" if you have ever bought a dog at the pet store at the mall because *"heeeee's sooooo cuuuuute!"* I wasn't planning to.

I always took my son to a hair salon at the mall to get his hair cut. While he was having that done, I'd take my 3-year-old to look at the puppies. There he was each time we went. Cute. Sweet. Pretty. Addictive. Every time we were at the mall, we'd visit the pet store and there he was. A very pretty Papillion, less expensive than the last time. Still prancing around with his head high no matter how long he'd been there.

It began when I Googled "Papillion." I think I was Googling for reasons *not* to consider him becoming a family member, but I couldn't find any. My son was by now *also* in love with him. He wanted him more than anyone else, but the answer was still no. Then one visit I felt my daughter's smitten smile spread to me as she

gently played with him. I realized that if I didn't get a dog, my little girl would not know having one.

I brought him home while their dad was out of the country. No notice whatsoever. Not even to myself. I did it before I chickened out. Of course he wanted me to return the little guy. Can you return dogs? I have never tried before or then. He was adamant, but I had a lot of ammunition in my corner to use. I reminded him of all the big decisions he'd made without me. I also reminded him that he was the one that put a doggy shower in when building our home when we no longer had a dog. He'd planted the seed. It grew.

This Papillion, Muffin. He's no Beau. But he's awfully sweet and cute and lovable and pretty. Even I call him a *she*. He is a yappy dog. He's my doorbell echo. In his little overprotective mind, everyone outside is there to kill us. I don't tolerate it well even after eight years, but hopefully my neighbors do. He took forever and a day to become potty-trained, which I found to be my weakest area of tolerance. He swallowed my daughter's first lost tooth. I did some excavating later that day outside to retrieve it. It was her first tooth

after all. He pooped on my kitchen table after jumping up there and

being stuck the whole day while I was out. Disgusting and hard for

me to divulge. He's peed on throw pillows on purpose. He's even

pooped on my bed.

This little guy sleeps with me in my bed most nights. As much as

he'd love to be king there, I won't allow it. I have to remind him that

he's just a dog. He states his disapproval with a loud sigh from his

tiny six-pound body. One recent morning, I discovered poop in my

shower. I guess he's picking up Beau's habit of avoiding carpets. I

always talk about finding silver linings, but it's hard to when you

find poop in your shower.

I get so mad. But then I look into those eyes. Innocence intensified.

Soul-saturation. Apologetically sad. And when I pick him up, he

tucks his head under my chin and reminds me that he's just a dog.

Lovable, poetically cute and pretty. And my daughter knows that

love. There are the nights when he sleeps at her feet, using his growls to keep her safe and separated from the night sounds. It makes it easier to forgive finding poop there. We are safer under his around-the-clock watch. I'm glad that he's here. He gives his little love so freely.

six

exes

I'm Knot Ready

My ex taught me to be un-anal without even realizing he'd done it. I was always being too safe about time, about tasks, and about being orderly and polite. The first thing that I found intriguing about him was that he always said what he felt. How unusual it was to me at the time.

I would rather bite my tongue, stay the safe route, not hurt anyone's feelings, sit quiet and worry what someone might think. I was not going to be the one to tell you something that you didn't want to hear.

How he said whatever was on his mind without concern of repercussion was the first thing about him that intrigued me into un-analness. The second lesson was how he would pick me up for a date, and then run a quick errand that he didn't get to that day because he had been bogged down with his work.

I remember thinking that maybe, just maybe, it's kind of insulting when a date wants to stop by his architects' office first before the restaurant. I'm sure my thoughts were, *why didn't he just let me know that he'd be a bit late and then do the errand without me?* Or maybe I was thinking: *isn't it a bit rude to make a date tag-a-long on an errand?* But then it occurred to me…

…he doesn't care what I think. What a wonderful idea!

Still to this day, I'm not sure if I should have been insulted or not, but back then it just made me think: *how cool would it be to not care what others think?* That would be so cool. So freeing.

I wanted to be just like him. I knew life would have a different feel to it if I didn't worry so much about others' thoughts and opinions and needs way more than I worried about my own. It's a habit not easily broken, but suddenly I had a window opened with lots of fresh air that wasn't there before, letting light in where there had never been light.

I dipped my toe into those waters slowly over the years, with cautious practice and indulgence. And now I rarely think about others' feelings until after I've said something. Then I might think, *maybe I shouldn't have said that.*

I've also learned over the years how to just let things go, which I now do with great success. So there's less worry, less safeness and less anal-ness in my life.

My ex helped me get there in other ways, too. I used to be *very* anal about keeping the house neat. I worked five day weeks in banking before I'd had my son and had created the habit of Saturday being cleaning day.

Nothing could interrupt my Saturday cleaning, even after I was no longer working. The cleaning just had to get done. Until he had an affair. Then it wasn't important. Nothing can compare to importance like the falling apart of a marriage.

So I worked hard to keep the marriage intact and it became my focus and the sponge of my energy. My son was barely two and my biggest focus and happiness in the years that followed, but the marriage suffered. I remember my ex mentioning to me that the house hadn't been its normal organized state for some time. I told him that when our marriage became organized again, I'd focus back on the house. I was okay with a messier house more than I would have been before. I wanted clean, but I wanted something else even more. I realized that the world wouldn't fall apart if the house wasn't in its place, especially if your world had already fallen apart.

I think he learned from me over the years, too. I know he had gotten lots of constant little reminders from me (smile), but one lesson stands out. When I got back to my anal household standards after my daughter was born years later, he had his decluttered house back again. My middle-school-aged son would come home from school and sit at the counter to have a snack with me before doing his homework. While we sat and chatted about his day, often times he'd pull off his socks and they would sit there on the floor after he went to his room. The house spotless, his dad would come home and see the dirty socks sitting amid the neatness. They would bother him so much.

He'd yell about those inside-out dirtied sports socks. He'd discuss them as if they were a creepy alien and it bothered me how much those socks bothered him. They were his pet peeve.

One day I suggested that he simply tell his son to pick them up instead of having a cow; it would be easier. But nothing worked to soothe his frustrations over the dirty socks. I sure wasn't anal about them. I'd learned so much in the past years that a pair of socks scored a zero on the one through ten difficulties-of-life scale. One day that I'm guessing he'd had too much coffee, he went way off about these socks.

The only response that I had left in me was, *"One day you're gonna' miss those socks,"* and I left him alone in the kitchen with them. He went quiet. He must have had a long talk with the socks and the two of them made peace. I never heard another word about them.

I know we can all look back on past relationships and appreciate the things that we learned from one another while there, no matter how much bitterness or anger occurred. My ex taught me to be real with myself and with others. I learned that I don't have to be so anal if I listen to my heart.

When it was time to ask for a divorce, I was thinking of me. I had kept things in motion for my kids, but it was time. He cried, but I was more in tune with the tears that I had shed. Without knowing it, he'd taught me to not worry as much about what others thought and to be more concerned about my own wants. He helped me discover that there are lessons to be learned in any circumstance and now I look for my lesson in all of my hardships and embrace them. And I know that I wouldn't be who I am, without having known him. All

of our relationships are valuable to us. Harvest and learn and love

and give and take from them.

Unguard

During Your Divorce

There's only one other person in your world that loves your children as much as you do. In the heat of divorcing them, it's hard for us to remember that one simple thought.

My ex picked my daughter up for breakfast one recent Sunday morning and I asked him if I could come along. I was hungry and dressed.

There is a restaurant that we both frequent with her, individually. Never together. It seems to be our favorite place to have a weekend breakfast, although between the three of us we've never discussed it.

The servers all know my daughters' order by heart; toast on the light side, crispy bacon, fruit and a side of cream cheese and a water.

We slid into a booth, me facing them, an image I don't see very often. Her eyes on her phone and her ears in our conversation. We had one light-hearted conversation after another with each other, and yes, our main conversation topic is and always will be about our kids, whether it's date night as husband and wife, or breakfast as exes.

A discussion about our absent 21-year-old son came up. My ex was already smiling huge about a seven year-old boy inside of a fourteen-year-old memory as he brought it back to life. It was one that I'd never heard. As he told it, his eyes filled with memory and liquid joy. It made his lips turn upward and his soft heart sit on his sleeve all wet and soggy. I took in the image innocently, happy to be on the receiving end. I tried to imagine what other memories might be ready to surface if I asked.

A drawback to divorce is that you don't have that person in your life anymore to reminisce about your shared treasures. It doesn't matter who comes into either of your lives. They won't feel the exact same way towards your children as you or your ex do.

In the beginning, divorce brings on foreign emotions; you've felt sadness before, but not quite like in your divorce. You've felt anger before, but never how it feels through your divorce. You've felt frustration before, but never, ever like in a divorce!

We had our ups and downs, but I still think we had a peaceful divorce compared to most. I attribute it to how we handled ourselves, not how we handled the divorce. It's *so* easy to become defensive, but we stayed on tract with who we were most days, and worried less about what the other was doing. We both had our son and daughters' best interest at heart, and that goes a bountiful long way in order to be able to deal and then to heal. My kids and I also stayed at our local beach house for the duration of the divorce.

I *highly* recommend a beach house (and wine and sunsets and walks on the beach and a lanai that is screened-in because mosquitoes suck, literally) for your divorce. It enabled me to have peaceful memories during some unpeaceful times. I was on "vacation."

I don't know if he ever hated me, but I never had a moment where I hated him that I can remember. And that helped when it was time to become friends again. Not the easy innocent friendship that we had when we first met and began dating. Not the committed friendship that we had while we were married. But a new friendship that makes everything bearable when you see each other all of the time for the rest of your lives because you have children together.

It's so much easier if you stay true to *you* while going through the throes of divorce because

at some point, you want to be able to look them in the eye again and feel okay about the past.

And it's okay to still be a support to your ex if the opportunity arises. You've shared a life together and cared about one another to great lengths in the past. What's one more time? And don't stand guard thinking your children need protection from their fathers' love. Allowing his love to flow to your children freely without standing in the way will only benefit your children. Step to the side and let him love them in the way that only he can. It won't be how you would do it but your children deserve the two different loves in their lives. And you won't have to do it alone.

January 23, 2001

Dear Sir;

My mother has just informed me that she has taken you back. You two seem to have an ongoing thing that I'd like to see come to an end. I recall the troubles of your last visit but I'm unable to convince her to leave you.

She is bringing you and her tender heart with her when she visits with me indefinitely. I can only sit by and watch her age as you intrude upon her life. The dark clouds will gather in her eyes whether we speak of you or not. You're her burden. While here, you will replenish your thirst with my water and your hunger with my food while I'd rather see you leave. She withers away when you're around. She's still the mom that I had as a child and is always able to impose her soft strength onto any challenge, but you make her weak. What hold do you have on her? How does she allow your feeble existence of life back into hers?

Regardless, I'll open my door to you both when you arrive hand-in-hand. I'll watch how you interact. She won't look me in the eyes when she's with you. It tells me that she doesn't want to discuss it. Her attitude towards you is so positive. She is a strong, kind and generous woman, but you have your toxic behavior and disastrous lifestyle. I wish you had more compassion. She doesn't speak of the dark secrets while living with you because she is too proud, but you provide the darkest moments of her 63 years. Your frequent traveling is important to your life, but it disrupts and limits hers.

If my mother is to rid you from her life, she has to be strong. When it's time for her to go home, I hope you will have already left without a trace as you have done in the past. It destroys her, but it's for the best.

There's a Light at the End of the Tunnel. You.

Please, Mr. Cancer, no more heartache and loss. If you leave, you

and your family will no longer be welcomed here.

Sincerely,   Katherine

[This is a piece I wrote thirteen and a half years ago when I was

caring for my mom during her cancer treatments and surgeries.

Unfortunately, my sweet mama had to leave before he did, but she

fought hard for the three and a half years he was with her. It's so

hard when someone leaves us, but I know that it's because they are

needed elsewhere. It's their time to shine some place new and

beautiful. God gathers us in so many different and difficult ways, but

in that brief moment of death and departure that forever scars us as

they leave us behind, they reach their peace and destiny. Let that

idea bring you peace and help you to reach your new and beautiful

place here.]

seven

the garden

The Garden

It starts with bare soil; quiet, cold and dark,

Unaware of the journey it will finally embark.

The seeds; full of hope, truth and light,

That begin to grow endlessly through days and night.

The water, the sun, and nutrients; plentiful,

The garden knows it will one day be beautiful.

One by one, buds appear slowly, without fail,

The roses bloom effortlessly and scent the air.

Damp from the rain and warmed from the sun, the seasons change

and pass,

The garden, it prospers; it chooses to last.

The thorns and flowers together demonstrate nature each day,

Once chosen, join together in one abundant bouquet.

A year has passed and the rose garden thrives,

It enhances the gardeners' love and their lives,

Always casting color and beauty and calm,

Almost as effective as a constant Song.

Katherine A. Rayne

About the Author

Katherine A. Rayne was born in Alberta, Canada and moved to sunny Florida as a child with her family. She freelances for family magazines as well as inspirational ones. She is a preschool teacher of the cutest little students. She founded <u>Back To Being A Woman</u> in order to support and inspire women to own their moments and find their light while in them. This is her second non-fiction book for encouraging women to live lighter and with less stress. She supports the idea that a peaceful home makes for a peaceful heart. She is a mother of two children: a now grown-up and warm-hearted son and an angelic daughter still with her in the nest.

www.ingramcontent.com/pod-product-compliance
Lightning Source LLC
Chambersburg PA
CBHW072009040426
42447CB00009B/1561